First published in Great Britain in 2000 by
TRIUMPH HOUSE
Remus House,
Coltsfoot Drive,
Woodston,
Peterborough, PE2 9JX
Telephone (01733) 898102

HB ISBN 1 86161 624 4
SB ISBN 1 86161 629 5

FOREWORD

Today, poetry has become a more recognisable form of expression and communication. Different styles are used by different authors; and from traditional to contemporary, all are included in this carefully and well thought out anthology.

Over 100 new and established writers featured in *An Open Faith* share their thoughts feelings and views with you, the reader.

With some of the best poetry emerging today we assure you that the book is an exciting and inspiring joy to be read time and time again.

Steve Twelvetree
Editor

CONTENTS

EARTH WAKES

Earth wakes
from the sleep of night
as the dawn sunlight
extinguishes
with living radiance
the glittering starfires
which lace the black fabric
of the sombre night . . .

At daybreak the kestrel
balances the wind
wings spread crucified
upon the cold hard morning air . . .

The bird is alone
in the empty sky of dawn
as the Earth spins
upon its invisible axis
while the human race
wakes sticky-eyed
to grumbling life
and harsh encounters
of the stress-filled
business of the working day . . .

But even now
mankind is reluctant
to shed the dream skin
of the snake of night . . .

Stephen Gyles

TIME

Across the bridge of time
I hear you call my name
Wait! Wait for me
You cry, and I shiver.

I feel your presence
And hear the seagulls' mocking laughter
As they soar shining silver
In the blue sky.

Love! Intangible! Untouchable
The wind and ocean hush
As we reach across time
To let our spirits touch.

Somewhere in time
Were we accursed
And doomed to live apart
In penance for some crime.

Wait! Wait you say
So I turn from others
Not knowing where or when
Or if we'll ever meet again.

Your voice and face invade my dreams
Though we are far apart
And should we ever meet by chance
I'll know! By eyes by voice and heart.

Then I will hold this precious time
Hold it! In the palm of my hand
Savour its sweetness like nectar or wine
For it may never come again.

Joan May Wills

EARTHQUAKE

Total eclipse,
Magnetic pull,
Gravity flips,
Tides go berserk.
Hush!
Night puts its lid
On flimsy man-made boxes
Built on a fault.
Suddenly a mighty jolt
Splits the earth's crust
Causing lofty buildings
That once stood erect
To nod their heads;
Tilt and topple,
Bite the dust,
Have domino effect.
Sudden death:
Shoddy structures
Become homespun tombs.
Infrastructure breaking up,
Pipes like serpents
Spewing mud;
Debris hurled.
Now survivors horrified,
Panic-stricken run amuck;
While women giving birth
Scream their babies into the world.
Over now! But in its wake,
Havoc, mayhem and chaos make
An act of God.

June Lane

BEYOND THE STARS

I know now that I have lived.

And if I never see another day as the last
sunbeam splutters from its fiery womb.

And if the Earth retch and spew
'til inside out and but empty shell.

And if the final rainbow unfurls and indigo
is no more.

I care not.

For I have seen the meaning of life.
In her gaze, bewitched.

Our eyes as one.
And all life's joy is squeezed in but
a single tear.

Time is no more.
A moment is infinity.

I ride the sunbeam from her smile.
Her eyes, a million twinkling stars.

I am hungry, yet filled; out-singing birds,
yet all is hushed; moved - yet unmoving.

I am glad to be a man.

And if we never meet again, I care not.
For one day she will join with me
as dust - whence we came; somewhere,
out there, beyond the stars.

And life will be once more.

Her eyes will light a new world; her warmth,
the sun; her smile - a rainbow.

And I will care.

Harry West

DREAMING THE DREAM

We dream the dream that never
unfolds,
That special event, yet to appear,
That over the hill is our pot of gold,
To make our life's purpose clear.

That one day all our needs will be met,
Waiting for the answers to our prayers,
Wondering 'why it hasn't happened yet'?
To lift us up from our worries and cares,

Financial reward to come our way,
At last, that dream to possess,
Something magical to whisk us away,
To bring the ultimate happiness,

Yet, while we wait for this big win,
The web of our future yet to unfold,
We wind the treads that start to spin,
The master plan yet to unfold,

The way we treat our fellow man,
Is one of the important ways,
To work ourselves into God's plan,
Making the best of every day.

Teresa Wild

AGE TWENTY-THREE

Bubbles burst and disappear,
Similar to life, ever so queer,
Here one minute, gone the next,
Three score years and ten the text,
Lives taken young and old,
Traumatised, body numb and cold,
Why has this happened to me,
Young man dead aged twenty-three,
A friend, I knew him well,
This illusive pimpernel,
Humour, the wit of a clown,
Macho, smart, a man around town,
Alcohol, the speed of a car,
A tombstone he went too far,
Passing his grave memories surpass,
Flowers surrounded by grass,
Imagination I can see his smiling face,
Halo there is no trace,
A young man now at rest,
Wishing him here to be my guest,
Sadly this cannot be,
His life ended aged twenty-three.

Alice Harrison

SEE GREEN

Help find the solution
to world-wide pollution
and give nature a hand,
every woman and man
please adhere to this plan
see green and understand.

Environmental health
must come first before wealth
most people would agree,
when you're not going far
try not driving the car
more cyclists we will see.

The time to deliver
and clean up your river
is overdue my friend,
we must keep water pure
or one thing is for sure
the world will meet its end.

All the fish from the seas
and the birds in the trees
were here before mankind,
if we refrain from greed
and let these creatures breed
more may be left to find.

Charlie McInally

SUMMER'S END

In a final gleam of sunshine
the trees stand motionless,
as if their prayers were answered
in the dying sun's caress;
while high above, scarce moving,
the clouds hang in the sky
as though they too were watching
the way the day would die.

The summertime is over,
and 'round us everywhere
the chilly breath of autumn
hangs in the evening air.
We face the approach of winter
with frost and freezing rain,
but we must wait with patience
for spring will come again.

Ivy Russell

THE ECLIPSE

Darkness, for but a fleeting hour. Power unknown dwells
high in the heavens.
The clock strikes and all becomes still.
The great creator moves at eleven.

Bright blue fades away, the sky turns to grey, as planets
align and revolve.
The birds cease to sing and still every wing,
a mystery no man can solve.

Silent in rows sit the old black crows, a still, leaden sky
broods above, and never a sound is heard all around,
yet the cosmos abounds, full of love.

Then bright comes the light as the diamond ring reveals
what the Lord set in place,
and back comes the day in its own blessed way,
see God's majesty, power and grace.

Richard Langford

A BRIDEGROOM'S PRAYER

I thank thee, Lord, for this my bride,
This dear, sweet creature by my side.

I thank thee for her face so fair,
Her laughing voice, her wayward hair.

I thank thee for her body fine
That yields so joyously to mine.

I thank thee for her loving heart,
I thank thee for her every part.

I thank thee, Lord, for this my bride,
This dear, sweet creature by my side.

John Watson

A CAMBRIDGE SPRING

There is a time when winter slips away
and Nature takes a canvas fresh and new -
Like college scarves the morning mist embraces ancient spires
and grass is shimmering with the sparkling dew.

Arrayed upon her palette Nature mixes them with care
the colours of her masterpiece for every flower to wear.
Virgin-white the snowdrops from their crevice peep
Beneath shadow of the hedgerow
Violets wake from winter sleep.

Upon the sloping riverbank and in the wooded glade
appear the yellow primroses emerging from the shade.
So silently and secretly these tiny flowers come -
With fragrance like a gentle kiss, seeking out the sun.

Next come the tall green heralds - in grass and on the hills
announcing that the spring has come -
the slender daffodils.
Like sentries stand the tulips of every tint and hue -
whilst bluebells weave the woodlands with tapestries of blue.

'Neath mullioned windows grey with age
the primulas display -
their jewel-bright colours to cheer the dullest day.
Pink and white the blossom floats on gently swaying tree -
delighting dancing butterflies,
sweet nectar for the bees.

Gentle chimes from college clocks ring out the precious hours -
from hallowed walls young voices rise
in praise of Nature's powers.
From budding trees a melody of birdsong gaily sing -
and Nature signs her work of art
and calls it simply - *spring*.

Iris Ashley-Grey

LORD OF MY HEART

Oh Lord of my heart I love thee
You're the sunshine on a summer's day
You're the birds that sing so sweetly
You're the laughter of a child at play

You're in the little dewdrop
Perched on the petal of a rose
You're in a fluttering white butterfly
You're in my garden, in everything that grows

Oh Lord of my heart I love thee
You're in the foaming waves of the sea
You're in the stars that fill each night
You're in the sweet honey of a bee

You're in each human emotion
You're in the hand that touches with love
You're in the soft white snowflake
You're in the peaceful flight of a dove

You're in the summer's night, cooling breeze
You're in the falling of the autumn leaves
You're in all the wonders that my eyes can see
Oh Lord of my heart, how much I love thee.

Susan D Williams

PRAYER FOR HELP

Lord you know all my needs,
Please help me as I plead,
Don't forsake me Lord I pray,
Watch and keep me all the way.

I know you answer all my prayers,
Guide and keep me all the way,
Lord you are my every need,
Keep me safe Lord night and day.

Shirley Lovell

THE TURNING OF THE EARTH

One awaits the moment of his rising
The dawn light is stirring - see, will he come?
Will it be where the sky is brightest
But lifting cloud obscures? Yet here he comes,
The brilliance penetrates above horizon's mist,
Cracks through the clouds, through twigs and trunks of trees
To reach the detail of our lives - arrives this day to seize.

And yet he does not stir.
By the hinging of the plain
Our whole county heaves the shoulder of the hills
The vale fills with his beams. In day we live again.

How can we face the light? Hold fast the rock
Vertigo o'ercomes us - cling to a stock
Say 'The sun, he rises'. We trust that we are still
The turning of the Earth is *not* done by *our* will.

Catherine Moody

AN EASTER MESSAGE

Jesus did not leave behind
the scars of his suffering,
He carried them to his risen life.

Not an end or a beginning,
love goes on and before,
we learn, grow and step forward.

We try to merge together
the cross of suffering and death
with the cross of life and hope.

Seeing our cross anew,
facing anger, violence and injustice
to give power to peace.

Holding before us
kindness, love and caring acts
without rejection or disparagement.

Learning and accepting that following
we must go ahead. We must use
the power of peace and love.

Fran Francis

CHRISTMAS

Put the Christ back in Xmas,
Have a good day,
With plenty of food,
And games to play.
Do all the shopping,
And watch the TV,
Use crackers for pulling,
And bring out the tree.

But stop and think
Of those who are old,
The needy, the homeless,
Left out in the cold;
The sick, the lonely,
Their solace is prayer,
Now on their own,
With an empty chair.

For Christ said whatever
You do for all these,
You do it for me,
And me you will please.
Put the Christ back in Christmas,
Have plenty of fun,
But remember the words
Of God's only Son!

Margaret Ruscoe

BE STILL

'Be still,' our Heavenly Father says,
'And know that I am God.
I know your hopes, I know your fears,
I know your needs, I know your cares,
Be still and listen to My voice
And in My promised word rejoice,
In weakness, perfect your strength shall be,
My grace your all-sufficiency,
Be still, My child, be still, believe in Me.'

'Be still, be still,' the Lord God says,
'And know My Spirit's power.
I know your frailty, know your sin,
I know your lurking doubts within,
Fear not My grace has set you free
From death the soul's last enemy,
My Son has paid your penalty
For this He went to Calvary,
Be still, My child, be still, just trust in Me.'

'Be still, be still,' the still small voice
of God is oft ignored,
The world's distractions ever near,
We listen with but half an ear,
Yet still He speaks and lovingly
'From sin and death I set you free
That you may have new life in Me.
Be still, My child, and know that I am God,
and in believing trust leave all to Me.'

Harriet M Seddon

QUESTIONS

Are you the sun to brighten our day?
Are you the moon to light up our way?
Are you the stars that twinkle above?
Whatever your answer, we're sure of your love.

Are you the breeze that gently blows by?
Are you the rain that falls from the sky?
Are you the snow that covers the ground?
Whatever your answer, in you love is found.

Are you the bird that sings in the tree?
Are you its song that brings pleasure to me?
Are you the flowers I see every day?
Whatever your answer, your love guides our way.

Are you the sea that rolls to the sand?
Are you the rock on which we can stand?
Are you the wind that travels so fast?
Whatever your answer, your love is to last.

Are you the stranger who's hoping to find
a hand that is helpful, a heart that is kind?
Are you the person who needs tender care?
Whatever your answer, your love we will share.

Cerys Hughes Taylor

REMEMBER ALWAYS

'Father, forgive. They know not what they do,'
Our Saviour's very words upon the cross,
Revive themselves, commandments which seem new,
Whenever we're reminded of harsh loss,
Caused by ourselves, or those just next in line,
Whose actions have a bearing on our cause.
We grieve by separations, that's sure sign,
Each one of us is closely linked by wars,
From which blood relatives did not return;
Great hopes, real talents taken before time,
So we have never known what some might earn,
And by their efforts, clean up that vast grime,
Of shame we have, on duty in their place,
Inadequately feeling, self-disgrace.
There are no methods known which could reverse,
These tragedies endured not long ago;
How many have not stopped to think, rehearse,
What they might ever say to some they know,
Who gave themselves, appropriately trained,
For fields of conflict far from what their youth,
Their childhood opportunities maintained:
'Here you may live!' Behold, that was no truth.
Disasters in man's heritage appear,
Revolving as a wheel. This does always
Require continual efforts: 'Look! Stand here!
There's danger any moment.' Which conveys,
Good orders of one kind to some who served,
Appreciating they were not preserved.
Now when we beg forgiveness for our past,
May we remember also, next time's cast.

Anthony J Russell

OUR LOVE

Love love love
The feelings inside we have with
Our love in our hearts
Love love love
We wait for the universe
To resolve or bring
Our love
We wait
Patience has to be kept
We wait
For our love
To survive
Love love love
We wait

Cynthia Osborne

FRIENDSHIP

Friendship is a loving gift
Not carelessly bestown,
And like a tender seedling
Needs care 'til fully grown.

At one time or another
Each one of us has sought
To find a kindred spirit
And share a dream or thought.

Someone who would understand
Without a spoken word,
And offer friendly comfort,
No silent cry unheard.

My friend you have given me,
In your own special way,
A constant, loyal friendship
Your gift for each new day,

In your supporting presence
Joy and sadness have been shared;
You have diminished heartache
By showing that you cared.

Joan Stangroom

ARROW OR TORTOISE?

When we pray with an arrow plea,
we are usually in desperation,
an immediate answer we hope to see,
as God comes to our salvation.

But sometimes the answer is slow to arrive,
God seems to ignore our voice,
no matter how we pray and strive,
God's answer comes on a tortoise.

But it isn't that He does not care,
or that we are somehow lacking.
Sometime or other the answer gets there,
the Lord still gives us His backing.

But in the time twixt prayer and grace,
our patience He may be testing,
or to see if our faith remains in place,
while on the brink we are resting.

So it's not that God is busy elsewhere,
or our sin has cut us off from Him,
but in patience our load we must bear,
while all around is growing dim.

For when that tortoise at last breaks through,
God's grace arrives with full measure,
the wait was meant to strengthen you,
and prepare you for stormy weather.

Prayer arrows bring you answers fast,
prayer tortoise teaches restraint,
both come from the Love that lasts,
and help us to become good saints.

Bill Hayles

MORE PRECIOUS THAN GOLD

He did nothing at all
That tiny scrap of humanity
To deserve anything so precious
So costly as gold.
Laid humbly on the bare earth floor
With frankincense and myrrh
It shone and glistened as it caught the firelight
Gold, the stuff of kings and princes
Freely given to this poor child
Sleeping under a silver star.
But, in a future time, as the sun's first rays
Dawned on another day
This same life would be betrayed for silver
And bring forth salvation gold.

Janice Lloyd

My Little Friends

As I wake up in the morning and look
outside
I see my little feathered friends come
down from the sky

They perch on my fence and wait for
the crumbs
And then fly down to take them back
to feed their little ones

I can hear the little ones singing in
the rain-soaked nest
And the mother is keeping them
Warm under her warm feathered
breast

It is 6 o'clock, and all is quiet
And I start to think of my little friends'
plight.
As they lay at rest inside their nest.

In the morning they are on my fence
looking for some crumbs
When they see the crumbs all gone
they all start bursting into song

I open my eyes and look outside and
I throw my friends some crumbs
They all fly down to take them back
to feed their little ones.

Bert Booley

CROSS AGAIN

Being on the conveyor belt at last
that is the way
applying it to others' needs
clarifies
that being off the way,
hitherto
I was,
if selfishly,
on the way.

Robert D Shooter

INTO THE SNAIL SHELL

You carry your house
Around on your back,
Never peeping out
You are worth the wants you lack.

Inside your protection
You fear a crack in the shell,
So scared to move
Your nakedness exposed as well.

You live life at a crawl
So scared to take a chance,
Slowing the pace of life down
To fit in with your dance.

A dereliction of duty
You're paralysed with fear,
So scared to move
The end is always near.

Inside your protection
You're scared to look around,
You fear a crack in the shell
Your house is falling down.

You carry your house
Around on your back,
Into the snail shell you retreat
You are worth the wants you lack.

Ian Barton

HELL

And who can tell
What is hell
But what we know of now.
      It is no worse
      Than the curse
      When sin did first
      Cast its spell.

The man who is estranged from God -
When someone asks of another he has met,
      'Where has he gone?'
Wise is the man to whom this
      answer belongs -
      'To hell - and not back yet.'

Sheila Seecharan

LA ROUNDE EN CIRCUIT

Warning: This I say: -
      always love your neighbour
              as yourself.
You do not comprehend what hence,
      if you do not:
if hate be the white-hot
ring of scathing fire,
yet truthful feel no actual depth repulse.

The circle is *you*: the nub
      of vicious sparks
sparing you no cooling path
      of safe return.
So intense the maxi ring!

As drips from heart
sweet acid deep
seeps throughout into the soul
the realm of love,
a love such tender agony to bear
a searing, tearing pain
much more complex than before.

Dorothy Mary Allchin

MILLENNIUM THOUGHTS

Two thousand years have come and gone
Since Light and Love lit up our earth,
And brought it warmth, with joy sublime
By Godhead suffering human birth.

From unimaginable heights
Of bliss and light, He stooped so low
That even angels stood amazed
To think that God could love us so.

But men, so foolish, sad, and lost
Did not perceive Him when He came.
Only a few folk recognised
His deity and Saviour-Name.

They're building structures up in town
To celebrate millennium year;
But few will understand His worth,
Or thank Him, just for coming here.

But some there are who bless His name
For all He's done to heal and save.
They've found forgiveness, peace, and joy,
And lost their terror of the grave.

These will be celebrating best
The life and death of Him they love.
His resurrection power they know,
And each new day His mercies prove.

But more than this, they're looking for
His promised coming back to earth;
When every wrong shall righted be,
And every tongue acclaim His worth.

Mary Pledge

DOES GOD EXIST?

Does God exist?
and while we mull away,
can human beings resist?

What is the grist?
wondering what to say,
does God exist?

Wandering through life's mist,
Satan holds fast his sway,
can human beings resist?

Where many Saints enlist,
he often wins the day,
does God exist?

It's best to be an optimist,
when evil has its say,
can human beings resist?

God can pass any test,
too many shades are grey,
does God exist?
Can human beings resist?

Jean Paisley

A FAMILY OF BUTTERFLIES

Lord, today I saw
a family of butterflies
in a field of sun.
They made me think of
dancing rainbows.
Prayers seemed to flutter among them.
Winds whispered on their wings
and I knew that only You
could create such a beautiful family
writing poems for me.

Marion Schoeberlein

GOD LOVES ME

He's a good God,
And wants the best for me,
Knowing God is the best thing in the world,
Have a relationship with Him today,
Tell Him you love Him.

Supernatural revelation,
Will begin to enter your life,
A positive kingdom will unfold,
To bring a beauty and eternal love.

Kenneth Mood

SHADOWS OF PEACE

In the shadow of Step Mountain
We shared our banquets
In the shadow of Step Mountain
We shared the Lord's Banquet
Neighbour to neighbour
Passing the Blessing, clockwise
In the Wee Chapel
     In the shadow of Skull Mountain
     Mystic darkness lasted
     A quarter's turn.
     The Cross was stepped up
     A quarter's turn.
     Pierced through *He* was
     With crude iron nails
     Pierced through *He* was
     With a sharp Roman spear
     Out of His death
     Flowed the river of life
     Obliterating guilt from our life.

Ron Cox

A WALK IN THE RAIN

A walk in the rain
All alone with your thoughts
In the forest
At the top of the hill
Pine trees and birch
Rhododendrons and ferns
Bramble thistle and holly
To reminisce of the times you have had
The good times the bad times
The happy times the sad
A walk in the rain
All alone with your thoughts
In the forest
At the top of the hill

Alan Green

THE PASSING HOURS

Heaven, I make my request - give to me a needed rest - fill
my hours with a peaceful sleep, although the passing hours of the
nights - ready then - to awake to enjoy the hours of the day - then may
I show the peace I have gained to other human souls on this planet
Earth - that it is good not to have to dwell alone - that my face will
show a contented smile - eyes ready to see the beauty that is always
there - whenever we may choose to gaze - no boasting ways or need
of clever words comes from Mother Nature's ways - only a willingness
to share the beauty - the wonders - of her silent ways - all this I
request - in the passing hours of my life - Amen.

R P Scannell

NIGHT

The shadows of night creep silently in,
Where does it end, where does it begin?
Everything is quiet and still,
The moonlight shining on the hill,
Stars light up the darkness of the night,
Each one a beautiful beacon of light,
An owl hoots in a nearby tree,
The wind gently blows across the sea,
The darkness of the night surrounds the world,
Far in the distance a noise can be heard,
Footsteps echo along the street,
Policemen are patrolling their beat,
Up the stairs we go on our way,
To sleep through the night to another day.

Sandy Grebby

MY GARDEN

To me a most wonderful place,
A place you can go and forget
All your troubles.
To let everything pass you by,
A place to go for peace and
Quiet.
And to pass the time of day.
To potter about planting this
And weeding too,
The flowers in bloom, their
Colours oh so bright,
And the smell of fresh cut
Grass,
Oh yes to me my garden is a
Most wonderful place, and
Such a delight.

William Livingston

THE WALK

I reach out my hand
But no one is there
Does nobody worry
Does anyone care

I was out on a walk
But I stumbled and fell
I've twisted my leg
And it's burning like hell

I look at the pavements
Deserted and bare
And down comes the darkness
There's rain in the air

I've tried to crawl
To a house or a place
Where I can get help
From the pain that I face

But I can't move my leg
It's swollen and sore
Can't someone please see me
From their front or back door

I look to the roads
But no cars passing by
I can shout to or signal
My distress to goodbye.

Ian Proctor

PAIN AND TEARS

All alone on that cross
He died just for you and me
To help bring us back to
His Father
So that we may be free

See the nails in his hands
The sinners laughed
And Thomas doubted
He hung on that cross
'It is finished' he shouted.

He lives in our hearts
Will reign there for
Evermore
The price he paid was
His life and for our
Sin he bore

James McCurdie

STEP INTO THE FUTURE

Let go of the past
you can't bring it back.
Your memories will last
when you want to back-track.

Step into the future
it's yours for the taking.
Let new hopes be nurtured
and new tracks be making.

The pain of what's gone
will soon fade away.
Create right from wrong
from this very day.

Smile with delight
at life's little pleasures
and happiness bright
will be yours to treasure!

Rosemary A V Sygrave

SPRINGTIME

Love is in the air,
Blossoms blooming everywhere
Makes us lift from our despair,
What a wonderful world,
We know the sunshine
Makes us smile, we hope
It's going to stay awhile,
We have so much to be
Thankful for, so let's say
Thank you to God once more.

Jayne Miles

SEPTEMBER

The first fortnight, the hottest in thirty years,
Wouldn't be surprised,
If next, it was announced to be
The wettest in living memory.

Most of the days were shiny and warm,
Only problem, less daylight hours,
Over which to enjoy or to keep out of harm
From any dangers which could happen to us or ours.

Next two weeks, entirely different,
Dark in the morning and wet,
Dark in the evening and still wet.
But, intermittently there was sun, so radiant,

It was easy to forget the wet.
On a happier note,
The harvest was reaped
Without too many worries to date.

The brambles though few,
Were not covered in dew,
The sun bringing out the flavour
In a way nothing else can endeavour.

The leaves on the trees are turning colour,
Autumn is in the air,
Leaves are falling everywhere
Ideal for the flower arranger's flare.

So, all in all, September has excelled
Our expectations and will be remembered,
Not least of all, for the riot of colour
Provided by the various heaths and heather.

Mary Lawson

THE BEGINNING OF THE END OF TIME

The world has gone awry
and soon all must die
For man has drained its source
now there's no time for remorse.
Its foundations have crumbled all away
no turning back the clock too late to
repay in any way.
He has cancelled future chances
as to the devil's music prances
He tried improving nature's beauty
which he mistaken thought his duty.
By greed, he never left well alone
desecrating earth that was his throne.
Time is all that man has left
all else! Bereft
Tho' he still had a thousand years
he may create a sea of tears.
He has no time to make amends
and he knows it is, The Beginning Of
          The End.

Agnes Burns Lawson

I'VE GOT TO GO BACK HOME

I've got to go back home.
I now remember her, long ago.
It seems so very obvious now.
There's just a thing or two to do,
Then I'll be complete,
I'll feel brand new.
I've got to go back home.
Some might say, to the other
Side of the world, to see
My Californian girl.
I've got to go back home,
To see my friend, buried beneath,
The winter snow, if, you're
Asking me about him, he died
Some time ago.
I've got to go back home
To respect his memory, now
He's left and blown.
I've got to get back home,
Back to Sacramento, to see my girl.

T C Maltby

BEHIND

Behind every cloud there is blue sky
Behind every sigh there is relief
Behind every tear there is joy
Behind every storm a calm

Behind every negative thought there is hope
Behind every night a day
Behind sadness there is happiness
Behind everything there is God

Behind silence there are words
Behind freedom there is a breath of air
Behind every death there is a new life
Behind every cross, the way.

Danielle Gallagher

ALWAYS

It must have been hard,
and yet you prevailed
through troublesome fates with whom you sparred,
the spiteful seas which you had sailed.

It must have been hard -
the roads which you dared,
raising us 'midst society marred,
shielded only by the love you shared.

We know it was hard;
so grateful are we
to the parents in whose life we 'starred' -
always in hearts' proximity -
always, though eyes may not see!

Perry McDaid

DISGUISE

Innocence paints pastel colour
Naive among the human jungle
Music imagery fills fickle minds
Unaware how reality may be unkind.
Maturity throughout the coming years
Lyrical tunes play no part to the ear
Reckless times seems more real
Hurtfulness many feel.
Reach height of life humble and wise
Alone or coupled without disguise
Only to wear comfortable smile
Which carries for miles.

Alan Jones

PEOPLE AND THEIR PRAYERS

People pray all the time, all over the world,
They all hope their prayers are by God Almighty heard,
And there are so many reasons for people to pray,
Whether it's the way they were brought up,
    their life circumstances or just faith - it's difficult to say,
Some people pray every morning - that's how they start their day,
For they want to thank God for everything that came their way,
The House of The Lord is a Church, people usually go there and pray,
But you can open yourself to God, regardless the place you are or stay,
The Lord is Almighty and listens to all of us,
People believe that He'll grant their wishes and pleas, so they lay in
    Him their trust,
I'm not sure if people exactly know how to pray,
First of all they should ask God for forgiveness
    for whatever they do wrong in their evil, sinful way,
But there's an important issue that people tend to ignore - I believe it's
    lack of understanding - what else!
To ask God for forgiveness - first they have to learn how to forgive
    themselves,
People seem to pray more if they're in crisis, unhappy or under
    enormous stress,
They pray to God and ask Him to guide them out of their personal mess,
Some people deeply believe that our Lord destines their lives, so they
    accept the Lord's choices,
Some people are even convinced that they're chosen by God and they
    hear heavenly voices,
Majority of people all over the world believe in Lord, our
    Almighty Creator,
Believing makes them strong, helps them to cope with life and what's
    more they really prepare themselves for the next life - later . . .
I think that through believing people not only purify themselves, but
    also, fulfil themselves mentally and spiritually,
And one can look at this matter from general point of view or
    individually.

Anna Bayless

LORD LEAD ME

Lord lead me to Heaven
Lord lead me to Your love
Please lead me to Heaven
To that wonderful home above

Lord lead me down Your pathway
Lead me to what You want me to be
Lord lead me in Your goodness
Until we meet in eternity.

Rebecca Jayne Williams

NATURE'S STORE

Food! How confused we are,
What is good, and, what is bad.
Count the calories, cut the fat,
It never mattered when I was a lad,
Stew with plenty of dumplings
Made with suet, by the way,
Built muscles and put hair on your chest
Or so my mom used to say.
And I can't remember a cow going mad
Stupid creatures though they be
Laying chewing the cud each day
More placid than you or me.
And whoever heard of a farmyard hen
Laying eggs that were able to kill
That little lion may have had something to do with it
Or putting the hens on the pill.
Fields and fields of cabbages, each one standing tall
Carrying its family of caterpillars,
They never hurt us at all.
Rules and regulations
Like we've never known before
Made by wise men to protect us
From the dangers of nature's store.
Could we please get back to the food God gives
Stop tampering with His perfect plan
You'll, maybe, not make so much money
But you'll be kinder to your fellow man.

Irene Spencer

REGULAR OR ROYAL

The best we wish to have
Is the same we should wish for others
Class and creed is a human design
The heart in every case, is really what should matter
Not blood, whether it is blue or red
God made us in His likeness - this we must remember

Peace is what we need, acceptance one of another
For at no time can we say, we have never done wrong, been wrong
Life is like a tug-of-war, we are always caught in a crossfire
It leaves us to battle on, to do what's right, to try and please everyone
It is at a time like this, we pray to God for grace
Grace to help in the time of need

Regular or royal, rich or poor, deep inside, we are all the same
We have the same needs, the same wants, hope for the same joy
Yet we *'dis'* others, calling to account their crimes
God gives us understanding, not to curse but to rally
Bear one another's burdens, the way Christ's love taught us to

Tomorrow have worries and anxieties of its very own
Sufficient for today, is today's own worrying troubles
Prayer, I offer to God, who sees and knows all things
The past, the present, the future, are in His hands
By His grace we stand

Regular or royal, we need to stand, linked hand in hand
In unity, in harmony, like a good melody, welcoming
The birth of a new century, for our actions count

Rosetta Stone

CONVERSATION WITH A GENIUS

'The difference between us,' the Poet said,
'Is that I hear voices in my head
That fill my heart up all the time.
I needs must write them down in rhyme
To let my soul fly free.'

'Oh I have those as well,' she sighed.
'Not all the time, and they don't bide
Long enough to memorise
And write them down for other's eyes
In prose or poetry.'

'What do you do with all your time?'
The poet, sneering, cried.
'Oh, other things, - aye there's the rub,
Clean and cook and sew and scrub
To keep you fed,' said she.

The Poet paused, - for once struck dumb.
Tears filled his eyes. No words would come.
She held him close and whispered low
'You're not the *only* Poet you know,
But you're the *best* for me!'

Heida

THE COME BACK

The people who rule the country
Are crying out with shame
They have encouraged
All the greed and laxity
And they don't know who to blame
They certainly have their problems
Should have known better from the start
While no good can ever come from evil
Shouldn't toy with the nation's hearts.

M Tickle

CHRISTMAS JOY

The workshop is so busy
Everyone has to lend a hand
All Santa's little helpers
In snow covered Lapland.
Everything has to be made ready
Before Christmas Eve
So elves and pixies
Must use their skills
And work with Santa
As there'll be stockings to fill.
So with nails and glue
They all know what to do.
Wooden toys and teddies
All must be got ready,
A large calendar on the wall
With a date marked
When 'Santa will call
So no tears are shed
From little beds
When children awake on Christmas morn.

Margaret Parnell

THE BUTTERFLY

A butterfly flew to a chapel today and carried the soul of my friend:
as I wept below she cradled the soul and whispered 'This isn't
the end:
come with me to the place you have seen in your dreams
where all those you love you will see,
your grief and your pain all fallen away, golden hours forever will be:
your memory remains with the grieving below
and as always with passage of time:
they will heal, and remember the chapel today
and your flight to God's golden design.'

A year has gone by since we all prayed as one in the chapel
and grieved for our friend,
I remember the colour of butterfly wings
and the peace with no visible end.
I'll endeavour to follow her footsteps
and live life as she would have done,
recalling how cheerful and gracious she was as each battle was won;
'Think positive' my friend would tell me: I know it's the right way
to be,
appreciate life's sweeter blessings and think a lot less about 'me'.

There is so much to do and so little time to live as we wish life to be:
just till a butterfly comes for a soul only this time she's calling for me.

Margaret McComish

DAY BY DAY

Spirit that blows through leaf laden trees,
Touch my soul within,
Take with you all my anger,
Weakness, doubt and sin.

Spirit of truth grace my mind and voice,
To speak as if to the Lord,
That my words shall not be regretted,
Or cut as the edge of a sword.

Spirit of will use what I am,
To the good, and not turn away,
For a helping hand I too may need,
Before the end of this day.

Spirit that lights my every day,
Shine strong on the pathways I tread,
Obscuring the dim and darker hours,
Until to His arms I am led.

J A Woodward

HOMELESS

Suna's winter fingers
Probe the frozen air
Revealing stranded traffic
Snowbound vacant stare

The chessboard comes to life
Burdened laden ants
Plod through drifts and slide
To daily working haunts

But those sunray fingers
Short-lived slowly turn
Now show the darker side
To humans of the sun

Lurking in the darkness
Nowhere safe to go
Nightlife of the darker side
Cold starved hours go slow

Mary Hudson

A PLEA

I feel your love
   I need your love
   Please come back to me
Why have you gone away?
I thought you were here to stay,
But when troubles came, you
couldn't take the strain.
But still I love you and
want to say,
Please come back again.

Jennie Rose Miles

OPEN DOOR

Ah! This place is so cold!
Flagstone floors, over which thousands of people,
some from far of places, have trodden.
Walls of solid stone, show the wear and tear of
centuries. Lofty ceilings protecting so many of
this cathedral's treasures.

Stain glass windows, windows fashioned by delicate
hands. Relate stories from the Bible.
It's June and the doors are flung wide open, it's
'Open Door'. For two weeks each year children come
from far and wide, to learn something of this great
cathedral.

There they are on their knees again, making brass
rubbings. Ah! well, one way of praying. Another
loving soul, patiently bending coat hangers. Showing
youngsters how to stitch and staff heads on puppets, one
of Bishop George Selwyn, and the Maori people of New
Zealand. Pity, though, half of them do not know one
end of a needle from another. What's that pushed halfway
under the bits and pieces? Dear me, better work
the lunch hour.

Wow! History brought to life and he knows his
Bible.
Newspapers, perhaps we will have a budding editor,
artist or reporter?
Delicate book markers. Tile rubbers, etc etc.
Drama, there's one way of bringing the Bible to
life. Especially when the youngsters have never
been inside a church before.

Thanks, yes, not in coinage but when one rascal
who has been particularly tiresome says 'Thank you
Miss for having me,' and they wave goodbye from the
coach. It's a good feeling.

Just wish we could have them more often
and then we could teach them about our loving Lord Jesus.
Never mind, the Holy Spirit is definitely working
amongst us, and the church is on the move.

Praise be to our blessed Lord who giveth all
gifts.

Maureen Margaret Huber

STAR

That star
Did not hang like a lantern
Over Bethlehem.
Having waited through aeons of time,
Anonymous among the constellations,
She was ready at last
For her famous appearance,
Trawling a trail for the Magi.
So much joy and excitement
Shook her fiery entrails.
'Make me invisible, sun,' she begged.
Unseen, she couldn't stay still,
Cavorted about the sky, bucking
Like an untrained colt,
So the planets, who could still see her,
Began to whisper reproaches,
So, slowly the star steadied,
So the magicians could find their way,
Then hung there, no longer invisible,
Like a lantern,
In the dark of the night.

J Bate

EARTHQUAKE

Terror unimaginable
Pain, agony unseen in darkness
Crying, screaming in horror circumstances
Bravery, desperate heartache
Death covering life in black holes
The moving hand through hell's dust
Walking wounded mesmerised
The world's professional help a must

Streets full of people where office blocks fall
Children lost to nature's awesome devastation
The broken city wrecked dreams
God taking fallen souls to heaven
In this hour of torment, past sins forgiven
Rescuers continue their terrible task
Among the thousands joined in death
The child pulled clear, saved, blessed

Many days now passed, more hidden life, little hope
Survivors struggle to reorganise shattered lives
No electricity, gas mains smashed
Polluted water, thirsting drinkers again risking death
Hospitals continue to struggle with the hopelessness
The awful stench of rotting flesh
Disease now rife, yet another claimer of life
Once the media moves onto tragedies new
How long will the outside world remember their constant strife.

Roger S Foster

I AM, WE ARE

I am, the morning, so clear, crisp and bright;
I am, the stars that glow and glint in the still of night,
I am, the erstwhile moon, that smiles a silvery white,
I am, the wind, which whistles through the trees,
I am, the golden and sweet honey made by busy bees,
I am, the early frost, plus or minus by a few degrees,
I am, the local news, shouted by the town crier, by his decrees,
I am, the badgers, hedgehogs, squirrels, active after the winter's freeze,
I am, the birds in light blue skies, gliding on the thermal breeze,
I am, the sun, so hot, so scorching, burning the bathers' skins with
ease,
I am, the children, playing on the beach, making sandcastles, crouched
down on their knees,
I am, the rain, lashing down, forming puddles, ponds, rivers, then
flowing into the seas,
I am, the clouds rolling by, drying the washing; to busy mums a sight
to please,
I am, the politician, engulfed in Parliament sleaze,
I am, the sheepdog, tending the flock, coaxing, nudging them into the
pen, I tease!
I am, the boyfriend, lover, always delayed, sorry I'm late Louise!
I am, that spring, that always pokes through, in those old style settees,
I am, the best cafeteria in town, I am called Betteas!
I am, the abominable snowman, my family in Nepal are called Yettis,
I am the museum and art gallery, I was once a passion of Paul Getty,
I am, the message of peace and world reconciliation, never short, long
or pretty,
I am, the warm tropical water, that laps against windswept jetties,
I am, the lion, elephants, wildebeest that roam the plains of the
Serengetti,

I am, the eternal optimist of all things, people's serene,
I am, all the world's best wishes, thoughts, their beautiful daydream,
I am, the final stitch in the tailor's seam,
I am, the dairy's milk of human kindness bottled topped cream,
I am, we are all, carriers of the future's many faceted main beam,
I am, we are all, God's multiracial, multi-facial creative team!
World peace, world without debt, hunger, war, it does not have to be
a dream!

John Cash

ETERNAL FLAME

You were the centre of my universe
The very core of my dear Earth
You gave my life some longed for worth
The dewdrops in a day's new birth
The rising sun, up in the sky
The rain that falls as if to cry
The stars that twinkle, far on high
Reflecting from the moon so bright
The clear, dark beauties of the night
Wonders all taken from my sight
You're gone, and nothing seems quite right
Though I've tried with all my might
Your face still haunts my day, my night
What happened to our 'eternal light?'
Did yours just dim or did it die?
But who am I to question why
I'm just the light you left behind
Your 'eternal flame' the one so blind.

Angela Maria Wilson

MY SOULMATE EVERLASTING

Although you seem so distant, your sparkle fills the air,
A candle flame still burning, waxing in the air,
I know you did not mean, to fill me with despair,
My soulmate everlasting, we'll meet again somewhere.

Paul Hanson

No Doubt

It wasn't my fault, I just didn't know
You could get a disease that for a while didn't show
Just one needle I did share
With just one guy, we were a pair
Then he got ill and he got too thin
And the agony, you couldn't touch him
His face it changed, all his hair fell out.
For this young man, who was once so stout
To every cold, bug or virus he was open wide
Only two short weeks ago, he died.
I kicked the habit, I said, 'No more.'
Felt rough for a while then found a sore
They spread round my body, I looked a sight
So determined this thing that I tried hard to fight
Weaker and weaker from day to day
A doctor was called and they put me away
Here I lie in this sterilised room
All shiny and white, but I feel the gloom.
I kicked the drugs right out of my life
A pain goes through me like the slice of a knife
I realise I have the fatal illness
From a long time ago, from my own carelessness
Just for the chance of getting a bit high
Now there's no doubt at all, I'm going to die.

S Eatough

A MOTHER'S PROMISE

I promise that I'll love you
I'll never cause you pain
The minute you're asleep, I long you
Both awake again
I promise to stand with you
Through all your walks of life
I promise to help and guide you
Through trouble and through strife
I promise that I'll nurse you
If ever hurt or sad
I'm your mother, you're my children
I will love you good or bad.

Glynis Whyke

THOUGH I'VE NEVER SEEN YOU

Though I've never seen you, Lord
Your image, is clearest in my mind
Your hands have moulded all of us
A universe and creatures of all kind

We have never stopped to wonder
The features - of the living things
Trunks and tusks of the elephant
All the birds with outspread wings

The snapping jaws of the crocodile
Ferocious - though they may seem
We have never stopped to wonder
How you've made man so supreme

You gave us a likeness of yourself
Gave some the power for to think
But do we visualise of the wonders
God could make vanish in a blink

Thank you Lord for the children
In heaven's light they are made
Make them honour their parents
And love in our hearts not fade

I believe, and have never doubted
You exist in some great off place
Where life moves on like a breeze
At ease, to please, heaven's grace

Robert Jennings-McCormick

LUCK

Is there such a thing called luck,
Or is it the way it's played?
The twists and turns of fortune
Can be tough or we've got it made.
Are we controlled like lifeless puppets
Or rollercoasting in a free-for-all?
Whichever line we take,
It doesn't make sense at all.
When we are young
The world lies waiting at our feet.
Fame, fortune and gold
Are the glittering goals we seek.
On the way, we, sadly, cast aside
The wholesome bliss of youth
For material things and thoughts
Forgetting one great truth;
What we sow we may not reap,
Life is fickle, like the wind.
Without warning, it blows hot, or cold,
We know not what it brings.
Luck owes no allegiance
To fact, fiction or common sense.
Its main function is to confuse us,
Forever, and ever, and ever.

Raymond Kirby

AS LONG AS YOU BELIEVE

I look into the moonlit sky
As I try to count my blessings.
I smile to myself,
For I know God is looking down at me
As I look back up at Him.

We are His children always and forever,
And I know that the brave Saint Peter
Will still be guarding the mighty gates of heaven.
I pray that is where I might one day go,
For as I write this poem I hope I am coming closer to God,
As I hope God is coming closer to me.

God comes in many shapes and sizes,
From a mighty, great tree
To an insect the size of a bee,
As I know God will be looking down at me.

The sun is His eye in the day
As the moon is His eye at night.
For He will protect me when I am sleeping,
As He will guard me while I am awake.

As long as you believe,
For you can be young or old,
Rich or poor,
The mighty Lord will have a place in His heart for all.

James Edward John Field (11)

MY PARENTS

When you are young you take for granted
In fact you feel that it is your due
Often you do not appreciate
All that your parents do for you.
But when you become an adult
Eventually you do realise
Some of the sacrifices they had to make
Then you view them with different eyes.
It was when I became a parent myself
That I finally understood,
Just how wonderful my own parents were
How generous and so good.
They had to make the hard decision
To bring our family over to Scotland
They had been forced to emigrate
I was too young to understand.
As we had all been born in Ireland
It was sad to leave all our relations back there
They had to make many more sacrifices
Their young family to rear.
We never felt deprived at all
It was always our parents who did without,
They rarely got new clothes, for example,
And never had nights out.
I always felt so loved and cherished
And we were taught to be kind and share
Though we never had much money
Our parents were always there.
I pay this tribute to my parents for the standards and set of
                                    values they gave to me,
Especially to practise faith, hope and charity.

Mary Anne Scott

More Than A Moment

I looked and saw the yellow rose
of peace dipped in blood,
it lasts more than a moment.
Children of men rage with discontentment,
it lasts more that a moment.
The whole world is going mad with
frustration to live,
it lasts more than a moment.
I say look for God, don't despair,
they look, for just a moment.

Kenneth Anthony

THE INNKEEPER

How could we know she brought the world to us,
And she just a girl, and tired, and near her time?
We turned them away. Was it so bad, our crime?
We had no room, and barely food to last,
So many people come here for the census.
Dear God, that we had let them stay that night,
And been His host, and welcomed the Lord of Light!
A child of the winter who gave the sun to us.
And afterwards, we heard when the Babe was born;
I remembered then a stillness so serene,
A gentle peace which held back the approach of dawn,
As if all time past and yet to be
Were encompassed in His hour of birth,
A sweet eternity that touched the waiting Earth.

Jacqueline M Atkins

THOUGHTS BESIDE LAKE VICTORIA, IN TANZANIA

Oh Lord! You made the heavens and the earth.
Such beauty and such wonder
And you said, 'It is good.'
Why did men disobey you and ruin your creation?
You made the rolling hills, etched against an African sky,
The glory of the flowering trees, blooming in profusion from a dry
                                        and arid ground,
And yet people are starving, children cry for food,
What have we done?
You made this lake, reflecting the blue of the sky, the rosy dawn,
Birds of many hues and wing spans,
The kingfisher gracefully diving to get his meal,
But the waters are polluted and crocodiles endanger children at the
                                        water's edge.
The massive boulders give a sign of your might, and brightly
                        coloured butterflies your artistic touch,
Such beauty and such danger.
You send the lightning that strikes suddenly without warning, and
                        the rain that pours out of a sullen sky,
But the rain does not know when to stop, and the crops are washed out.
Great areas of parched land still wait, and the crops wither and die.
What have we done?

Joy Tilley

CENTURIES

Throw off the crown of thorns my Britain, Church, Monarchy and State,
The thorns of politics never made a country great!
Only festering sores, scrapes, predators clamber through,
Church, politics piously proclaiming! Protect Monarchy,
'Let her rest in peace,' Monarchy burn down your
Thorny hedge, leave all charred sticks behind,
Protocol forsake, proclaim to your seeking nation,
'In Cloud-Cuckoo-Land we will live no longer,
'You placed us on the throne, we will put you first,
Leading into a New World of love, peace, righteousness,'
Our Parliament with a smile will kiss you, clap their hands,
'The thorns pulled out healing our aim too,' they say,
Use these instruments in Ireland, blooms of peace
Blossoming, roses, shamrocks, heathers, daffodils,
We cannot do without each other in our green Isles,
The burnt thorns disintegrated into dust,
The Head once crowned with men's thorns,
Is crowned with God's everlasting glory now,
Jesus' cry, 'Tis finished,' was not what man thought,
But a New Beginning, He rose on Resurrection morn,
In love He is still begging, hence happenings of these days,
Let the World cry, 'Great Britain has the answer,
We will follow them, God's way,'
God did not send St Paul west for nothing,
Join History's Celebrations, not it wakes and dirges,
But the third millennium entered in jubilation as the first,
'Hallelujah!' cry Church, Monarchy, State, Peoples . . .

Anne Mary McMullan

THOSE WERE THE DAYS

I remember the winters of yesteryear
when the house was bleak and cold.
There was no central heating
and the rugs were pricked and old.

Bathtime was strictly once a week,
We never had a phone,
Washing was always done by hand
but Mother never moaned.

We didn't possess a Hoover,
Dad swept dust under the mat.
The bed was really cold at night,
We often wore a hat.

But Santa would always come,
Stockings were always full.
We had so many happy times
that life was never dull.

Christmas Eve! How exciting!
We'd gaze out at the stars,
I could swear we heard the sleigh-bells
echoing from afar.

Although our lives have changed,
I'm sure you'll all agree
there's nothing like the good old days
to share a memory.

Wendy Watkin

CARE OF US

Do not weep
For this has to be

Oh! How hard to part
For, this breaks my heart

But! We all grow old
Become ill and tired
Our bodies are weak
Yet the spirit's strong

'God' will take
Care of us
When the time comes,
Along.

Gladys Davenport

THE MILLENNIUM CALL

Two thousand years have passed and gone
since God our Father, sent His Son.
A little babe in a manger laid
His mother, Mary and Joseph too, and many
angels, yes they knew, that
Jesus had come to share our life.

His Father loved us all so much,
and longed for our return.
Mary, Joseph and angels all,
listened, lived and answered the call,
The way that leads from death and sin.
The way is clear, for those who will hear.

It is the Lord, the Beloved Son,
Just follow, listen and you will see,
Along the path He will be there,
For He is deep within you,
Listen, trust and you will see
the road that leads to eternity.

The Father's Son, the Beloved One
is longing for us all, yes, you and me,
To leave the sin, the self, the all.
Come listen to His Glorious Call.

Sister Etheldreda

A FARAWAY FRIEND

I'm so often in here hiding
behind these stone cold walls,
feeling only desperation, as life
around me collapses and falls.
Such despair of facing another long day,
which brings nothing but trouble and strife,
angry pent up emotions within myself.
Where did I go so wrong in my life?
Until within these walls a voice I heard,
so serene stirred thoughts within me.
An American lady on a talk show
seemed a friend was reaching out you see.
'When there's only darkness in your life,
that's when you look to the stars'
Her words seemed to inspire yet soothe me,
to look at life beyond these prison bars.
As evening fell I promised myself I'd go
sit beneath the stars,
to maybe find fulfilment that I seek,
beneath Jupiter, Saturn and Mars.
Peace I've now found beneath midnight skies,
turned my back now on trouble and strife,
I cope so much better with life's ups and downs,
now I've got peace of mind in my life.
How I'd so like to meet the lady whose wise
words reached out to me,
to thank her for being the inspiration I needed.
A friend she always will be.
'When there's only darkness in your life,
that's when you look to the stars.'
'Yes' - my faraway friend.

Michele Simone Fudge

ETERNITY

He who blinds to
himself and joy,
Does the winged
life destroy;
But he who kisses
the joy as it flies
lives in eternity's
sunrise.

P Pattil

JUST A DAY OUT

Woke up on a cloudy day
'We'll go to Southampton'
He was heard to say
Only twenty miles, not very far
Get yourself ready
We'll go in the car
On arrival we paid one pound
At a *'Pay and display'*
We had quickly found
Given three hours to explore
Just another sixty pence
We could have had four
First we walked the city walls
Stood gazing out to sea
Caught an open top bus
To visit Town Quay
Round and round the bus did go
Couldn't get off
At places we didn't know
Finally begged the driver
'Please open the door'
Sped to the car park
Sacrificing rest of tour
There sat our car, we sighed with relief
Till we saw the envelope with letter brief
A £30 fine they kindly gave us
If only we had skipped the open top bus
Even more sense
We should have paid
That extra sixty pence.

Brenda M Hadley

SPECIAL FRIENDS

Special friends
Are very hard to
Find
So please keep
This in
Mind
When looking
For that special
Person
Whether it's a
Husband, wife
Or even
God
Is our friend for
Life
But not a
Foe
And who can
Ask for
More

Coleen Bradshaw

NONE SO DEAF

They tell me I've got 'depression'
They're clever, so they should know.
I've got lots of tablets that make me feel worse
And if I'm no better I'll soon need a hearse.
My Fred popped his clogs, and the children have gone
I'm lonely, not ill, when I tell them so
They don't listen.

We used to live in King Street
With friendly folk all round
They sought cups of sugar, and stayed for a chat.
But never come near my tower block flat.
A social worker comes to call
But she doesn't stay long, and has no
Time to listen.

The children phone to tell me
Of holidays abroad
They are too busy to visit me
I cut the apron strings, they're free.
And though I'm pleased that they're content
I miss them, and I tell them so.
They don't listen.

Muriel Berry

OUR YESTERDAYS

Those were the days, I hear people say
Remember as if it were yesterday
No running water, an old tin bath
Outside loo, down garden path.

Corner shop, goods on tick
Penny for a fag, made you feel sick.
Coal in street, horse and cart
Walk to work, for three thirty start.

Gas lamps lit, streets at night
Surrounded by smog, dimming the light
No tele, car, or washing machine too
Just a dolly tub, ponch and a bag of blue.

Nit nurse called at school most days
Teachers were strict, with caning ways
School bobby cycled around the street
He'd chastise, any child he'd meet.

Dad did wear, hob nailed boots
visit pawn shop, to pledge his best suit
Those were the days, I hear people say
Thank God, those times are over
As we relive our yesterdays . . .

GIG

MOUNT TIEDE

She stands there, with her whitened brow.
Mount Tiede
The nearer you get she seems to grow.
Mount Tiede
Smooth and tall and proud she is,
Men dig their heels and spikes
in climbing, rather cruelly.
But she puts on her mantle of the ice and snow
And makes men think, it's dangerous there to go.
There she stands proudly showing off her charm,
Men will not break her, or ever do her harm,
She will retaliate, and those that know
Have seen her fury, and the heated love flow.

B Puddefoot

INTENSIVE CARE

Eerie vault, the colour of snow.
Weary mind, a yen to go sledging
on Blueberry Hill. Dark sound
tearing at the ears (might have been
laughter, but too many fears
come tumbling after). See, hear, smell.
That's all. Walls of silk, like
an open coffin. Would-be mourners,
like milk bottles on a doorstep
that someone forgot to cancel.
Kind words, a constant hum
carving me up for the family album.
Would pray, but nothing comes of trying,
only pain - and a question of dying
best left unsaid, so back to sleep instead
and chance waking up again
for a general examination of my flaws.
Angels pause to peer in my face,
bid for my soul

What *is* that smell? Sanctity or cruelty,
I know it well

R N Taber

LAMENT

Chaucer, Shakespeare, Milton enduring sublime
Were special seeds maturing with time;
Meter, simile and grace of rhyme
Germinating with lavender, rosemary and thyme.
Keats warbled as a skylark sings
Hopkins raged as a nun to wreckage clings.
Before watery Motion swims shimmering rivers
Coleridge's sleep evoked dreams in shivers
And Tennyson versified all that entered his head
And dallying Dylan sang of Swansea and lava bread.
Others grieved about soldiers in battle
And of illness, hospitals and the death rattle.
The moderns pictured like a Lowry painting
A landscape dull with commercial tainting.
Whatever the source that springs the poet's muse
The very truth sparkles in words they use.
Much may be left for me to say
But I remain in frustrated disarray.

Leslie Johnson

THE GOOD SAMARITAN

Samaritan neighbour, chosen by Christ
An example to all who live in this life,
A vibrant, considerate, thoughtful man,
You took on yourself a sensitive role
To succour a needy and ill-fated soul.

You offer mankind a superlative way
Respect for life and realist thinking
By helping a man who was left lying dead,
You gave new life and uplifted his head,
Redeeming his life by giving your own aid.

By pouring on oil and tending his wounds
You showed true compassion and honour too,
Unlike the others who passed by on their way
Regardless of how they really could help
They walked on to Jerusalem to comply with their laws.

But you, O Samaritan showed a real aspect of love
Devotion to duty as sent down from above.
Your courage and mercy in face of adversity
Was truly surpassed by your wonderful pity
You helped - that sufficed - the man lived again!

Thanks to you Samaritan neighbour, example for us all
Of love and devotion and sensitive thought.

D T Beeken

THE WANNABE

When I was 4 years old they asked me:
'What d'you want to be when you grow up?'
'A priest' I said.
Oh, my father's eyes!
But I had glimpsed my soul's purpose
To be a holy man.

When I was 8 years old they asked me:
'What will you be when you're grown up?'
'A writer,' I said.
Oh, my schoolmates' sniggers!
But I had glimpsed my soul's purpose
To be a teacher of men.

When I was 12 years old they asked me:
'What d'you want to do when you're older?'
'Be a doctor,' I said.
Oh, my teacher's face!
But I had glimpsed my soul's purpose
To be a healer of men.

When I was 16 years old they asked me:
'What is your chosen career?'
I just lied.

F A Materski

HALLOWED BE YOUR NAME

I hallow and bless your name, O God,
With every passing day. But how arrogant,
How smug this sometimes seems to me. For how can such as I,
A creature of your creation and recipient of your grace,
Be worthy of blessing you, the God of all.
How insignificant is our blessing in the light of your goodness.

My child, a blessing of itself is empty, devoid of matter.
Words that mean nothing if not evidenced by deeds.
I crave your blessing, my child, I yearn for your response.
Yet it is not your fine words that I seek, no matter how oft repeated.
It is to see your response to my love and care
Reflected in the way that you treat others.

All my children need my love and care - they have it -
Free of any demand for payment.
Yet even by blessing can seem worthless
If it is devoid of tangible support.
I gave myself on the cross for all, of every race and generation.
Now it is through my faithful children
That my ways are made known.

Bless me, my child, by blessing others,
By loving them, by serving them,
As they are, not as you would have them be.
They are my children and I made them as they are -
It is through you that they will come to know my ways
And understand them.
Then will I be truly blessed.

Peter Scares

DOWN TO EARTH

People are warned, to stay out of the sun,
And just like steaks, they get very well done,
Turn them over, and baste them with oil,
Then lightly touch them, and watch the recoil.

As they pass by, out on the street,
Can't you just feel, the output of heat,
Gritting their teeth, to hide the pain,
Every year, over and over again.

Staggering about, with arms spread wide,
Agony, when brought down to their side,
Cannot bear the weight, of light summer things,
Put on some soothing cream, it really stings.

Why do they, torture themselves so,
Just so that they, can have a nice glow,
They worship the sun, but it does not care,
Burning relentless, as if no one was there.

Heatstroke, dehydration, damaged eyes,
And because of a hole, in the skies,
Ultraviolet, tempts the romancer,
The only satisfaction, is a skin cancer.

Robert Thompson

MADE IN HEAVEN

I have a story I must tell,
Of once upon a fairy tale.
The stories told by birds' song high,
Of the magic from the sky.

A coin she threw in waters white,
To wish for happiness in the light.
The water sprite for he did tell,
A tiny sparrow at his well.
Fly over her with rainbow bright,
Let her dreams be peace tonight.

A kindred soul she will meet,
One day upon a busy street.
There fall in love beneath your home,
No fancy place but grass and stone.
Fairy lights will dance and fly,
As the sea meets the sky.

The sparrows in the treetops sing,
Of a pretty rainbow ring.
And of her love for they have told,
How he made a band of gold.
Then plucked a star from the sky,
And in the magic of an eye.

He held her hand to his heart,
And whispered they would never part.
He asked if she would be his wife,
Two souls to love for all their life.
Hearts and souls now at rest,
Because they know it's heaven blessed.

S Rafferty

EVENING

Oh God, we love the twilight hour
The skies in red and gold
Dark shadows of the evening
Softly come and interfold.

We love the wild flowers shutting
Their petals for the night,
To open in the morning
Brought out by bright sunlight.

The miracles of nature
Are ever with us here
Trees so tall in statue
And skies so blue and clear.

The Lord who made creation
In perfect harmony,
He gave the sea its limits
And the earth, fertility.

M Morris

LIVING IN THE NOW

A wise old man once said to me,
That there is no time. Which I failed to see.
There's only *now*. Then that time's gone
from whence it came, and no more shall come.
Only the moment is forever here.
Past and future are never as clear.
They're only memories, and some - perhaps.
And, the truth's unclear in those mishaps.
Only in the moment, is what is that's true.
Distorted not, by a wider view.

Why waste energies, on what's yet to be?
Which can change in an instant, as your will is free.
And, why waste energy, on what is past?
That changes nothing, and will only last.
If you yourself, dwell on these things
Focus instead, on what the now brings.
By doing this, dealing with each moment in hand,
whether good or bad, you'll soon understand.
And are able to cope, with all that seems sent.
Each moment is now. So, make it well spent!

With his words in mind, I altered my course.
Made each moment count. Without any force
I took what came. Addressing it head on,
there's nothing to fear, as my fear has gone,
of what past I recall, or what may yet to be.
Living in the now, has set my soul free.

Christine H Goldsmith

THE BATTLE

Fight all evil with the love of God
Who permutates your being
As He looks upon your daily life -
All powerful - all seeing.

For those who hurt with hand and tongue
Are blind to our God's love -
Who longs to be accepted
As He reigns in heaven above.

Jesus Christ within your soul
Who died and rose again -
Will be very evident
If a Christian you remain.

Put on the truth of armour
And beware of evil's cunning
As you fight with Prayer and full of Peace
To see the Devil running.

No matter what befalls you -
If injured in this fight -
You have entered into eternity
And faultless in God's sight.

The Holy Spirit left you
By our Saviour dear and true -
Will guide you through these coming days
And make them bright and new.

Pat Melbourn

MAN'S SIN

God does not make war
So cry not out, obey his law
Ten rules he commanded us to bide by
We broke them all, you and I.
With free will he allowed us to dwell
In a paradise we turned into hell.
God showed his wrath, he was angry with us
In his sorrow, he sent down his son Jesus
To teach everyone how to give, love and pray
We crucified him, so ended his stay.
War is created by men to serve greed
God takes no part, it was not what he decreed.
Thou shalt not kill, is one rule of the ten
We all bear the guilt of millions of men
Killed in man's war, and women with children flayed
Tortured and maimed, degraded, raped, betrayed.
So cry not out to God, don't call on his name
Until man wars no more, we all live in shame.

E Merritt

A GRANDMOTHER'S SMILE

A little girl knelt by her grandma's chair,
A lot of things they would often share.
A lot of things she did not understand,
So gently she took her grandma's hand.
Grandma why do you always smile?
Do you get lonely, once in a while?
Because dear child you brought me joy,
Just like your father when a boy.
Seeing you playing happily on the lawn,
I may be alone, but I'm not forlorn.
Many's the happy hour I've watched you play.
You're my sunshine come what may,
Your tears only come when you fall,
And I'm here when you often call.
The smile on my face is what you bring,
With your laughter and when you sing.
A smile may come from the heart,
With a love that never falls apart.
A smile of joy, the happiness I want to show,
For the loveliest little girl I know.

Margaret Upson

LET JOY BE OUR ISSUE

If I had a song to give to the world,
It would start with a woman's heart.
To grow with each child, no matter how wild,
As their experiences turn wrong into right.

Sometimes over the years, days dark, tears and fears,
Make our closeness become, deeper love, next to none.
They struggle as teens, through puberty, causing scenes,
And when the other sex draw, bring romance to our door.

When at last they arrive, with that first grandchild,
All that remains is the joy, not the pains.
Now through it all they must go, and the wrinkles will show,
The downs to frustration, the ups to elation.

K P Watch

MY GARDEN

A garden is a sanctuary - all one's own,
A garden is a haven for all things grown,
Vegetables, flowers, shrubs and trees,
It is also a place where one's found on knees,
Grubbing out the weeds, cultivating too,
A garden returns rewards - just for you,
Colours abounding - perfumes strong,
One could remain in a garden - all day long,
A garden is a place of safety - from most foes,
Why even there are thorns - to protect a rose,
For safety there is no better place to be,
Ouch! I've just been stung by a bumble bee!

John L Wright

TO THE DOCTOR

Unexpectedly
our paths crossed in third world country,
another language
a different culture,
bearing upon you heavily
the onus of your
extended family
whom you see occasionally, fleetingly,
constantly working
dawn till night, high moon,
never forgetting
to tend sick infants in commune,
without charge,
in gratitude of triple bypass success
a silent vow made by you to Allah if blessed.

In contrast you were amazed I stayed,
Europeans
usually
continue global holiday
instructing to send body home if battle lost,
astounded and ashamed that some count monetary cost
I said nothing.

What do we know
of the inner man
until we pause and learn?

Hilary Jill Robson

FREEDOM'S LAUGHTER

Through rising mists their laughter sounds
For freedom they have attained.
No blood was shed, none lay dead.
And still the battle won.

As the Israelites in the days of yore
The Scotsman now is free
Free from the English tyrant sword
To fulfil his destiny.

So if ever you're in Scotland
Walking through a highland glen
Don't be dismayed at sounds you hear
It's only freedom's laughter, floating in the air.

S Banjona

FULFILLING LOVE AND LIFE

Love - to me that once in a lifetime - finding a true friend,
My feelings, my worries they understand, always seem to comprehend.
Love is to make the most of life, not waste a precious moment,
Grasp with both hands the gift of life, to the bad things not relent.
Love is sharing, caring, giving - to those who share your heart,
Achieving working together, listening, and hoping never to part.
Love is appreciating the glory, the natural beauty of all around,
For true love of life - heart - and mind will always astound.
Love, a feeling of peace, tranquillity, understanding, being complete,
At times things going wrong, right words not found, being discreet.
Strive to achieve what everyone wants, from this Gift without strife,
For to receive and accept peace of mind above all -
                                         is the meaning of life.
We all at times carry a cross, so often we think too heavy to bear,
When we received life, it was a lifetime given - a venture to share.
Love is taking life seriously yet, sometimes taken as acting the fool,
Sometimes listening to the heart, not always letting the head rule.
Above all strive towards perfecting one's beliefs, and what love is,
Then love will be fulfilling, rewarding and life not an unending quiz.
We are only on this planet once - however long or short the time,
Time enough to look inside - say this is my life full of love - it's mine.

Irene J Mooney

IMPRINTS

The clay upon my thumb
Takes the imprint of the skin
And flakes away.
The coal upon the fire,
Imprinted tree,
Moves into flake,
And I sit in my chair,
Imprinted me,
And stare into the fire.
Thumb round my chin,
Feet on the floor,
I see the fallen clay,
The dust within the grate,
And wait on time.

Stewart Gordon

GUARDIAN ANGEL
(Dedicated to Matt - I'm sorry)

A confidant, a friend.
A helper when I was in need
Someone to save me from myself.
Someone who needed to be helped
Someone who needed to be protected
This someone needed helping more than I did
Yet I never knew this and put myself first.
Now I blame myself for the silence from them
I never listened to their cries
When they needed me I wasn't there
When they were always there for me.

I could never have imagined
I never would have guessed.
I'll never understand, because I don't know them;
Anymore.
I once thought I did
But now I know I was never even close.

Hannah Shooter

INFORMATION

We hope you have enjoyed reading this book - and that you will continue to enjoy it in the coming years.

If you like reading and writing poetry drop us a line, or give us a call, and we'll send you a free information pack.

Write to :-
Triumph House Information
Remus House
Coltsfoot Drive
Woodston
Peterborough
PE2 9JX
(01733) 898102